Finding a Job in the 21st Century

How to Find a Job (Without Losing Your Frickin' Mind)

by Benjamin Paul
Publisher, Job Samurai

Published in USA by: Job Samurai

Benjamin Paul

ISBN-13: 978-1-970119-29-9

ISBN-10: 1-970119-29-2

Table of Contents

About the Author

Benjamin Paul is a former recruiter, corporate trainer and career coach.

His mission in life to rid the world of bad interviews (even worse resumes) and help job seekers around the world find the career of their dreams.

Prologue: "We're Not in Kansas Anymore"

"The only way to make sense out of change is to plunge right into it and join the dance."

-Alan Watts

This book will not tell you how to format your resume.

Or how to write a cover letter.

Or how to network at a job fair.

Or how to fill out your 295th job application on Career Builder.

There are plenty of books out there — some of them good — to tell you how to do all that stuff.

I know, because I've read them all.

I found out what color my parachute was — magenta, it turns out — and I memorized all the job seeker "best practices" out there.

Such as:

- How to hide a total lack of experience on your C.V.
- How to "follow up" with a hiring manager with this handy-dandy "email template."
- And what to do when you get fired from your job at Sea World for throwing a churro at a costume character dressed like Shamu. (True story.)

Here's the thing, all those best practices might have been what you needed in the Mesozoic Era. (You know, back in 2002.)

Things MOVE faster now. You don't have time to "wait" until the interview to show you're the perfect candidate and have all the qualifications they're looking for.

You'll never get in the door. (Or even the waiting room.)

You've got to ESTABLISH yourself as a kick-ass candidate and industry heavyweight, beforehand. (Relying on a single-spaced one-page resume in Times New Roman font won't cut it.)

That's the bad news.

The good news is…

It has NEVER been easier to increase your visibility, boost your credibility and claim your rightful place as a kick-ass ninja in WHATEVER field you're in. (Or want to be in.)

Don't worry if you don't know your Facebook from your Twitter-verse, I will walk you through it, every step of the way.

Trust me, I'm no social media expert. If my wife "checks me in" at another restaurant on Facebook, I will throw something.

I am, however, a fan of technology that "works"

for me while I'm sleeping. The kind that does all the networking for me while I catch up on all those back episodes of <u>Breaking Bad</u>.

So…I know you're skeptical.

I know you've already made a list of all the reasons the strategies in this book won't work.

That's okay. Hold on to the list. Heck, keep adding to it, if you like.

Just put a modicum of faith into the strategies I outline in this book.

Not because I'm some best-selling author or professional speaker…

But because I've used these strategies to get interviews which turned into jobs.

And it can do the same for you.

Modern Job Search or The Art of Herding Cats

There's an old saying from P.T. Barnum, yes, the

circus guy.

He said, "Half of all the advertising I buy is a waste of money. Trouble is, I don't know which half."

I don't know which technique or strategy you use will be the one that will unlock the door and help you get that job of your dreams.

If you're responding to every job listing you see on Monster, CareerBuilder and Craigslist, keep doing that.

If you're calling up every recruiter in a 90-mile radius, keep doing that.

If you're walking around downtown with a sandwich board that says, "Will Web Design for Food," keep doing that.

The strategies in this book will not only support and augment your existing actions - 'cept for the sandwich board one, but...

They will also do the most remarkable thing...which is to make the whole process of applications, resumes, cover letters and phone

screens irrelevant.

You're about to make the transition from the PERFECT candidate to the ONLY candidate. I feel sorry for the competition. They have no idea what's coming their way.

So if you're ready to become an unstoppable force of non-sucky 21st-century career awesomeness, turn to the next chapter and let's begin.

Chapter 1:

The Ultimate Jedi-Mind Trick

for Job Seekers

"Help enough people to get what they want, and you can get anything you want."

-Zig Ziglar

There's a nasty little secret all those companies and businesses you're applying to don't want you to know.

And that is…

They need YOU a hell of a lot more than you need THEM.

I know you don't believe me.

That's okay. I wouldn't have believed me either.

I figured the reason I wasn't getting any bites on my amazing chronological resume was because:

- The economy sucks
- Nobody is hiring
- I didn't have the right skills
- I was too qualified (Or under-qualified)
- I was cursed by a Romanian witch during my trip abroad
- I'm just no good

I'd still be stumping around all those soul-crushing job fairs if it wasn't for my cantankerous, old Uncle Lou.

He explained over a couple of Miller Lights one night — "None of that German import beer junk!" — that my job search would not REALLY take off until I could see things from the perspective of those hiring me.

See, Uncle Lou had started, ran and sold 12

companies in his 20 years of business life.

He had hired and fired more people than Donald Trump. (He had better hair too.)

He knew about water filtration. Asian imports. Car rental franchises. Luxury sporting goods. Car dealerships. English pubs.

The man knew business.

He knew employers and business owners had THREE major thought processes going on in their brain when hiring staff:

- **No.1: They WANT to Make Their Life Easier** (That's Why They Want You!)
- **No.2: But They Don't Want to Feel Dumb** (And Nothing Makes 'Em Feel Dumber Than Hiring a Schmuck)
- **No.3: So, It's Better to Hire a Safe Candidate (**Than a Rock Star Candidate Who May Disappoint)

Do you know how stressful and time-consuming

it is to rifle through piles of resumes and anonymous online applications?

They WANT you to be the perfect candidate. Mostly so they can stop the "hiring" process and get back to work, but they're afraid they'll make the wrong decision.

Which would set them back even further and make them feel not-so-good about themselves as a business mogul.

So…they rely on time-tested (if arbitrary) considerations like:

- Prestigious educations
- Advanced degrees
- Letters of reference
- Previous experience
- Unique skills
- Industry certifications
- Common associates and friends

When all they want is to find somebody who'll a) do their job and b) not screw them over and make them look dumb.

The reason "networking" is so powerful isn't so you can show how awesome you are at collecting LinkedIn contacts.

It's SOCIAL PROOF you aren't a sociopath which tells employers they can feel "safe" in bringing you on the team.

So…how does this change things for us?

How can we use this handy-dandy insight in our job search?

Well, before we jump into the nuts-and-bolts job-search strategies — and I've got lots of 'em for ya — I'd like you to make a subtle shift in your approach.

As you go through all those job listings, online applications and interviews I'd like you to ask yourself a simple question: "What can I DO for this company?"

Instead of thinking - "Boy, this job would really help me pay off my car loan" - try to see it from the employer's point-of-view.

And ask, "How could I kick some serious ass for this company and make them look superb?"

I know…sounds super new-agey and artsy-fartsy…

But there's something about this that works. Asking these simple questions:

- Makes the whole job search feel less personal
- Gives you a lot more confidence and motivation
- Fills your brain with positive questions, instead of the usual: "Why am I so sucky at this?"
- Makes you super kick-ass during the job interview

I know it sounds stupid. It is stupid. But it totally works.

And I can SAY the moment I focused on this one concept…things started to pick up for me.

Don't worry: in the next chapter we'll get less Tony Robbins. Promise.

Chapter 1 Key Takeaways:

- **Employers WANT to hire you**. They're just terrified of making a mistake.

- **Resumes and job interviews are just ways to reduce their fear** in hiring you.

- **Ask: "How could I help this company kick ass?"** during the job process will boost your confidence, motivation and results during your job search.

Chapter 2:

6 Pillars of Job Search

Awesomeness

"A ship is safe in harbor, but that's not what ships are for."

— *William Shedd*

Before you can run, you gotta learn to walk.

And before I show you all my ninja tricks for finding companies and employers who are bat-poop crazy for not hiring you — we've got to make sure you're ready to capitalize when you make contact.

Some info in this chapter may seem simplistic.

(Most job-seeker books spend 300 pages on the perfect resume. I'm gonna try to handle it in under 300 words.)

You may already know you shouldn't have pictures of you smoking a joint on your Facebook profile.

But trust me, this stuff is REALLY important. Skipping any of the steps in this chapter can disrupt your job search. (Which leaves you filling out applications down at Home Depot.)

So, here are my 6 Pillars of Job Search Awesomeness to Get You Primed and Ready for Killer Networking and Total World Domination:

Job Search Pillar No.1: A Somewhat Rough Idea of What the Hell You'd Like to Do

If you're zeroed in on your industry, then skip on over to Job Search Pillar No.2.

But if you're NEW to the job market, or you're thinking of changing careers, then you might be unsure of what KIND of job to target. (Let alone what you'd like to do with your life.)

This will be a matter of choice, but let me give you a couple of questions to ask yourself:

What am I already **GOOD** at or what do I already **KNOW** other people don't?

Make a list of your skills and areas of expertise. (Even if you don't think you want to do it.)

Just because you hate working in a call center doesn't mean you wouldn't be a good fit in a marketing firm elsewhere. You may just need a change of scenery to help you use the skills and talents you already have.

What do I really care about?

I can't guarantee you'll be able to get a gig around your passions. (I'm still hoping to play shortstop for the San Diego Padres. Yeah, don't think that's gonna happen.)

But if you can SOMEHOW link up your passions with an area of business, you'll not only have an easier finding a killer job…but you'll be enjoying it much more.

What am I opinionated about?

Check your Facebook feed and try to figure out - what forces you to chime in and share your opinion? Is it local politics, animal rights, children's issues, health & fitness, or that horrible Michael Bay movie you saw last week?

I did this exercise with a friend who scanned his Facebook activity and realized what he REALLY cared about was income inequality. (Lot of that here in Southern California.)

It focused his job search and helped him land a

gig with a non-profit that aligned with his interests.

I know this sounds silly but linking up PASSION with SKILL is one of the most powerful things you can do to boost your job search.

Job Search Pillar No.2: A Killer Resume (That Doesn't Scare Off Employers)

Entire books have been written about resumes — Amazon boasts 600 different options for you to choose from — so I will not try to compete with those worthwhile resources.

But having created over 150 different resumes and having hired 30 people in the last year, here are a few things I've learned about the good old Curriculum Vitae:

- **Nobody cares about your objectives**. Kill that boring horse-dung paragraph where you tell me what YOU want. Boring. Get to the stuff us hiring folks care about.

- **Instead, focus on a "Summary of Qualifications."** Tell me how your skills tie into my objectives as an employer.

- **Emphasize SKILLS over JOBS.** I want to see what you know, not which business park you parked your car in for three years.

- **Don't be married to the WHOLE CHRONOLOGICAL thing.** It's not THAT important. Nobody will check if you left any jobs out.

- **Tell me your achievements, not your job responsibilities.** I don't care what you did every week. Tell me the kick-ass things you accomplished in each job. If specific revenue was attached — "I sold 45 million dollars' worth of fresh lobster out of the trunk of my car" — tell me!

- **Get them keywords in there**. Figure out the common "keyword language" of the industry you're in — or want to get in to — and use those keywords throughout your resume.

- **Keep it short**. And cut the "references available upon request" part. We know they're available.

- **Do a different resume for each different ROLE you think you might be qualified for.** One of the (first) smart things I did in my job search was to create a separate resume for the different jobs I was interested in. (Example: social media marketing, content producer, search engine optimization, shortstop, professional Xbox game tester, etc.)

Job Pillar No.3: Take Your Killer Resume Online

Okay, so now you've got your resume(s) looking awesome, it's time to take them on the virtual road.

One of the coolest places to do this is a website called About.me. It's free, it's easy, and it's a great way to create a visual resume that highlights your skills, accomplishments, and (best of all) personality.

But that ain't all!

You also get a custom (friendly) URL that you can share with your contacts. (And add to your business card.)

You also get some analytics to find WHO is checking out your resume. (And you will get people checking out your resume.)

Job Pillar No.4: A Sanitized Social-Media Footprint

Since I started my business a year ago I've hired nearly 30 employees. Know the number one thing I check before setting up an interview?

It ain't their references or their LinkedIn profile or their work history.

It's their Facebook profile.

Whether you realize it or not…the stuff you (and your friends) post in your Facebook newsfeed has a DIRECT and significant impact on your hire-ability.

Now, I'm not asking you to join a convent or take a vow of social-media celibacy.

Just realize that those pictures of you downing a shot of tequila with a sombrero on — "What happens in Vegas, usually ends up on Facebook" — will come to haunt you later on.

This also applies to the photos, videos, and links you SHARE in the newsfeed. Save the overt politics and NSFW videos until after you've got the job of your dreams.

Until then: keep it rated PG and with no references to religion, politics, or Lady Gaga.

Job Pillar No.5: Set Up Profiles on All the Major Job Search Sites

I know you've already spent some serious time on many of these — likely with a little luck, if you're reading this.

But don't worry, I will show you how to change all of that.

Until then, you gotta have a presence on all the biggies. And that list can change from time-to-time. (Oh, how we miss you, Yahoo Hot Jobs.)

Here is a link to an article (JobSamurai.org/JobSites) that profiles the biggest job search websites. (It includes biggies like Monster, Indeed, CareerBuilder, and some I had never heard of.)

The key is to fill out a profile wherever possible AND include "industry keywords" that recruiters and hiring managers can find you with.

Most hiring managers are lazy. I know, because I was one for years.

Make their jobs easier, by adding all those keywords, and they're more likely to bring you in for an interview.

Job Pillar No. 6: A Place to Show Off Your Expertise (and Your Personality)

I know what you're thinking: "Isn't my resume the place to show off my expertise and personality?"

Nope.

The resume is just a sneak peek. A 30-second trailer. (And not a great one at that.)

It ain't the movie. It ain't the full-on two-hour

epic saga that shows prospective employers three major things:

1. This person CARES about something besides their paycheck
2. This person has some serious initiative
3. This person would be a KILLER addition to the team

The best way I know how to do that is to create a website or blog that is solely dedicated to you and your professional brand.

Before you freak out and say: "I don't know my HTML from my JavaScript flash proton torpedoes."

Don't worry, this ain't 1998.

My 75-year-old mother has a blog. And she's a woman who refers to Mark Zuckerberg's social networking company as "The FaceBlock."

If she can figure it out, you can too.

Which is why I'm devoting the next chapter to your internet hub of blog awesomeness!

Chapter 2 Key Takeaways:

- **Ask questions to figure out what do.** Focus on what you're passionate about and, what you already know to see where those attributes might make a good fit.

- **With resumes - keep it short**, focus on the skills and accomplishments, add lots of keywords, create different resume versions, and forget that boring "objective."

- **Create a virtual resume at a place like About.Me**. Then add that resume URL to all your online profiles and business cards.

- **Clean up your social media reputation** BEFORE you start the job search. You need not be a monk, just ditch the party photos and controversial status updates until after you have the gig.

- **If you haven't already, set up a profile on all the major job search sites**. Don't forget to include your different resume versions.

Chapter 3:

Conquering the World One

Blog at a Time

"Much unhappiness has come into the world because of things left unsaid."

-Fyodor Dostoyevsky

I can just hear you now…

A blog?

"But I thought this book was supposed to help me with my JOB SEARCH. No-body said anything about a BLOG."

And your objections are valid. They (probably)

include:

- "I don't have time to blog"
- "If I did have time, I'd have no idea what to write about"
- "Doesn't everyone and their grandmother already have a blog (that nobody reads)"
- "Did I mention I'm the world's WORST writer on the planet?"

You're right. Most blogs suck. (Mainly because people post twice and then forget about it.)

And they do require a SLIGHT amount of actual…you know…effort. (But less than you'd think.)

And MOST blogs comprise people whining and/or sharing everything that happens to them, like some extended Facebook status update.

But that's not what YOU will do.

You will create a small little hub of content awesomeness where you share digestible, bite-

sized portions of all the stuff you know and have learned.

We do this because:

- Broadening your job network on social media is a HELL of a lot easier if ya got content to share.

- Writing regular content (stuff focused on helping others) is the EASIEST way to position yourself as an expert (no matter what the field).

- Writing regularly on any given topic will keep you engaged and plugged in to your industry. (Might even lead to a whole new career you never thought of.)

- You MIGHT not make money as a blogger until your REAL JOB kicks in. (Not a lot of moolah, but maybe some burrito funds.)

- You can put down INDUSTRY BLOGGER as an occupation on your resume if your C.V. is skimpy.

- If you believe in karma - and I do - then giving back to other people is a fantastic way to let the universe know you're ready to accept a kick-ass job.

I know you'll resist this. You'll be tempted to skip this step.

That's okay. I was resistant too.

I can tell you from absolute personal experience that the moment I wrote (regularly) what I knew and gearing it around what might help other people…

That's when all those LinkedIn groups, Twitter followers, Facebook friends and YouTube subscribers I had morphed into genuine career leads.

In the midst of the worst economic downturn in the United States since the Great Depression, I found myself with many job offers.

So, try it. It's worked for me and everybody I've worked with. I know it can work for you.

It's About the Blog, Stupid

Creating an authority blog is simple:

1. Create a blog
2. Make your blog not look super sucky
3. Brainstorm topics to cover
4. Commit to a regular writing schedule
5. Write the posts!
6. Publish the posts!
7. Promote the posts!

Once you get your blog up and running, none of this should take more than an hour a week.

What else are you going to do?

Update your Monster profile…again?

Watch another episode of *The Real Housewives of Modesto*?

Trust me: doing this will make you STAND OUT from the rest of the job seeker schmucks. So, let's break down these blog-creation steps a little further:

Authority Blog Step No.1: Create Your Blog

This is the step most people freak out about. Which is weird because it's the easiest.

I mean it, you need NO technical skills to create and maintain a blog.

The only real question to ask yourself is, where the heck is my blog going to LIVE?

You got lots of options. They include:

- Blogger
- Typepad
- Tumblr
- WordPress

My preference is WordPress. For a couple reasons:

- **Even though Google owns Blogger, they LOVE WordPress blogs**. Meaning your blog has a good chance of showing up high in the search-engine rankings.

- **WordPress has a lot more features** than Tumblr or Blogger.

- **You can ADD an all-important sidebar widget in your WordPress blog** that tells people you're available for hire AND Where they can see your visual resume.

To create a blog on WordPress, all you have to do is:

1. Go to WordPress.com
2. Click "Get Started"
3. Fill in your info, including a NAME for your blog.

The hardest part will be coming up with a name. This will depend on your own style and personality but try not to go too crazy.

Try including the main keyword of your industry — (marketing, financial planning, Go-Go Dancing)

— and try on a sexy content word like *tips* or *secrets* or *101* or *guide* or *insider.*

Authority Blog Step No.2: Make Your Blog Not Look Super Sucky

I'm no graphic designer, so if you're looking for professional web design tips you've come to the wrong place.

If you're using WordPress, much of the actual design or LOOK of your blog will be determined by the THEME you decide to go with. There are lots of FREE themes, just Google "Word Press themes" and you'll find a zillion.

No matter what your blog LOOKS LIKE the most important part of your blog is the "sidebar widget" that "gently" reminds readers you're available for a job and where they can get more information about you.

To add this (in WordPress) all you do is:

- Click on "Appearance"
- Click on "Widgets"
- Drag one of the "Text" widgets (found on the left side) into either Sidebar 1 or Sidebar 2. (This will depend on your theme.)
- Paste your job search info into the "text widget"
- Click Save

That's it! Su-uuuuuper simple.

So what do you put in that text widget? Well, here's what I put in there that helped me get a ton of responses:

"Looking to add a kick-ass social media marketing expert to your team? (Who also makes a wicked espresso?) Check out my resume at http://about.me/Michael457 to see how I might be able help your company or business reach a whole new set of eyeballs you never thought possible."

Now, you'll want to tailor it to your own

personality. My blog posts were cheeky, so the "espresso" thing fit in just fine. (Although steal that one, if you want.)

But notice how my blurb stresses how my qualifications are tied to the goals of a prospective business. (It ain't just what I can DO…but how what I can do can help THEM. Simple, but important.)

Authority Blog Step No.3: Brainstorm Topics for Your Blog

Once you've got your blog set up, it's time to come up with some stuff you will fill it with.

And though you can share personal things from time to time — I wrote a post once about how I was looking forward to the zombie apocalypse — mostly you will want to write content that actual humans want to read.

And the number one thing people want to read about is STUFF that helps them answer

questions and solve problems.

Finding this stuff is easy. All you have to do is:

- **Make a list of all the stuff/topics you know about.** We already started this in the last chapter. For me, my list might include: social media, writing, home video, blogging; email marketing, etc.

- **Come up with FIVE additional sub-topics related to those bigger topics.** For example, "social media" would suggest Facebook marketing, LinkedIn Groups, Twitter, etc. "Writing" would suggest, writing grants, freelance writing for magazines, copyediting, etc.

- **Then take each of these sub-topics and do the following Google searches**: 1) "how do I" AND [sub topic] 2) "why" AND [sub topic] 3) "what" AND [sub topic].

- **Scan the Google search results** and see what interesting QUESTIONS come up.

- **Compile the most interesting questions** into a spreadsheet.

Seriously. Do this and you'll NEVER run out of stuff to write about.

Authority Blog Step No.4: Commit to a (Regular) Writing Schedule

Don't freak out. I'm not gonna ask you to write blog posts six times a day. (Like I used to have at my old job.)

Once a week should be fine unless you want to write more. If so, knock yourself out.

Don't feel like you have to write a 1,000-word epic every day. (200-300 words are more than fine.)

Just make sure you pick the day(s) of the week you'd like to publish then stick to it repeatedly. This will help readers, get used to your content schedule.

Authority Blog Step No.5: Write the Posts!

Want my best advice about writing blog posts? Don't write them.

People get in trouble when they start "writing." Instead, think of your blog posts like conversations.

Like "talking" with a friend who you're trying to explain a somewhat difficult concept to.

You could:

- **Sign up for a FREE Google Voice account**. Then call the number and leave a message which will be transcribed and sent to your inbox.

- **Use the FREE vocal transcription software on your PC or Mac**. These are not always accurate, but still is way better than not writing.

- **Talk into your smartphone recorder**

for a few minutes and then transcribe the audio later. Or if you got a few bucks, you could hire somebody to transcribe it for you.

And as for the actual form of the blog post, here's what I do every time:

- **Scan your list of sub-topic questions and pick one**.
- **Come up with a title based on that question**. The words "how to" or anything with "numbers" work. Something like: "How to Get More Twitter Followers" or "3 Tips for Getting More Twitter Followers."
- **Write a couple of brief sentences describing the problem and what your post will cover**. "Getting Twitter followers can confuse and, if not done right, can lead to your account getting banned. Here are 3 Tips to help you get

more Twitter followers…"

- **Write the meat of your blog post answering the main question.** "Step One: Follow the Twitter accounts of people whose followers you'd like to connect with. Step Two: Don't be an asshole…"

- **Write a recap that gives people steps they can take**. "So to recap, here's what you do…"

And that's it! This should take about 20-30 minutes.

The most important thing is to tell people, right up front, WHY they should read your blog post. (And then give 'em the information you promised.)

Authority Blog Step No.6: Publish the Posts!

How to do this will depend on the actual blog

platform you go with.

If you choose the WordPress universe, it's simple:

- Log into your WordPress account. This will be: "http://yourblogname.wordpress.com/wp-admin.
- Under the "Posts" tab on the upper left side, click on "Add New."
- Fill in your title, blog text and tags (insert the sub-topics your blog covers).
- Click "Publish" and you're done.

Yes, there are a ton of other things you can do with each blog post, but you ain't trying to conquer the Google monster or become a world-class blogger.

You are just creating a content hub that will show off your knowledge and expertise.

Authority Blog Step No.7: Promote Those Posts!

Once you've published a blog post. It's time to SHARE it with the world. And turn all that wonderful content goodness into job prospects.

That process begins in the next chapter!

Chapter 3 Key Takeaways:

- **Creating a blog is easy**. WordPress is the best, most versatile platform around.

- **Your blog's design is not that important.** What's crucial is to have a sidebar widget that lets people know you're available for a gig and how they can view your resume.

- **To find topics for your blogs posts** just brainstorm a list of sub-topics, then do a Google search to find out what the FAQ are about that sub-topic.

- **Try to write a blog post at least once a week.** Remember, try to shoot for the same day each week.

- **Structure your posts by following a simple formula**: Intro, how-to, and action steps.

- **If you HATE writing, try TALKING**

your blog posts instead. They might end up being better in the long run.

Chapter 4:

Your Job Search, 140

Characters at a Time

"The secret to getting ahead is getting started."

-Mark Twain

And you thought Twitter was just a place to find out what pointless, rambling thought Kim Kardashian shared with the world?

Twitter is a fantastic way to galvanize your job search.

Because Twitter is:

1.   **Super easy to use**. If you're a total

social-media newbie, Twitter is a great place to get the hang of that whole social media thang.

2. **Most of it can be automated**. Meaning you don't have to spend all day checking your Twitter account. You can actually do most of the work the day or week before.

3. **Fast**. That 140-word character limit (now 280; but I encourage you to still keep it short) means you can plow through a ton of tweets rapidly.

4. **Great for getting to know what a business is like**. One of the best ways to investigate prospective companies you're interested in.

5. **Easy to make an impression on**. Most people suck at Twitter. Being even remotely interesting will make you stand out.

6. **Where most companies post open**

positions. Forget those stale "careers" pages, Twitter feeds are where most job listings show up first.

7. **Where lots of recruiters hang out.** I'll show you how to find all those recruiters later on in the chapter.

So how do we turn all those tweets and retweets into an actual job lead?

Well, here are my FOUR PILLARS to help you maximize your Twitter Job Search:

Twitter Pillar No.1: Create a Twitter Profile That Doesn't Suck

Signing up for a Twitter profile is dead easy. Just head over here.

Making sure your profile is complete and does all the work for you it can isn't as easy.

Remember, your Twitter profile is like a super-enhanced virtual business card on

steroids. So little details, like the profile photo you choose or the username you decide on, make a difference.

Here's what you need to know about rounding out your Twitter profile:

- **Try to get your REAL NAME in your Twitter username**. It's not always possible. At least avoid creative flourishes, such as StreetNinjaz43, and keep it connected to your given name.

- **Get your job pitch in your bio**. Your Twitter bio is valuable real estate. Tell people who you are and what you're looking for. Personality is always helpful. "I'm an Austin-based web developer looking for a new opportunity that incorporates my two loves: programming and strong coffee."

- **Get job keywords in your bio, if possible**. Notice how I got "Austin," " web developer" and "programming" in

there. That wasn't by accident. Any
recruiter searching on Twitter for
"Austin web developer" has a good
chance of finding me.

- **Include a link to your virtual resume
  in your bio**. Remember that online
  resume I asked you to create? Well, your
  bio is a perfect place to put a link to
  your virtual resume. Convert the link
  with a shortening tool like bit.ly and you
  can track how many people are clicking
  on your resume.

- **Upload a great Twitter avatar to your
  profile**. You'll want a square headshot
  for this one. (No distance shots.) The
  max size you can upload is 500x500, but
  the picture will size down to 73x73, so
  you'll want to make sure the image is
  clear at that size.

Twitter Pillar No.2: Follow the Right People (and Companies)

If it's true it's NOT about "what you know" but about "who you know," then no tool helps you boost the amount of WHOs you know, than Twitter.

Here's how I would suggest you approach your job search on Twitter:

1. **Make a list of companies you might have an interest in working for.** Start with at least 15-20 and build out from there. Add companies even if you're not sure if they have a position for you. Don't limit yourself.

2. **Follow the OFFICIAL Twitter accounts for those companies.** This will give you not only an insight into company culture but also give you access to job postings when they happen.

3. **Follow the hiring folks for all of**

those companies. Just head over to Twitter advanced search. And plug in the "[company]" — along with phrases such as: *hiring manager, recruiter, recruiting, HR* — in the "any of these words" field.

4. **Follow any general job listing Twitter accounts**. (Mashable has a GREAT list here (JobSamurai.org/TwitterJobs) of Twitter profiles that might be worth following.)

5. **Follow any relevant regional job listing Twitter accounts**. Again, the Mashable list is worth looking at.

6. **Follow any industry-specific or trade association Twitter accounts**. See the Mashable list.

7. **Follow recruiters in your area**. Again, head over to Twitter advanced search. And plug in YOUR city in the "near this place" field — along with phrases such

as: hiring, recruiter, recruiting, etc. — in the "any of these words" field.

8. **Follow recruiters in your industry**. Same drill. Head over to Twitter advanced search. And plug in your industry in the "this exact phrase" field — along with phrases such as: hiring, recruiter, recruiting, etc. — in the "any of these words" field.

Twitter Pillar No.3: Give, Give, Give….Receive!

Here's how most job seekers use Twitter:

"Hey everybody. @LoonyBoy here! Anybody know of a job opening. I have no skills, little experience. But I'm hoping you Tweeps can help. Plz!!!!!!!"

Yeah. Just makes you want to jump right off the couch and help, right?

The (sad) truth is that most people consume Twitter while they're on their smartphone. Meaning they have the attention span of a gnat while they look at your desperate tweet.

And they're looking for two things:

- Things that are interesting
- People they know

Your job, as a Twitter job seeker, is to leverage BOTH while not alienating people by being too personal and needy.

So, here's my handy-dandy little formula for WHAT to post on Twitter:

- **20% Inspirational quotes**. These are like crack on Twitter. People love 'em. So why not give it to them? Just Google "motivational quotes" and you'll find millions.

- **20% Cool industry blog posts and/or articles.** What kinds of articles you share will depend on your industry. But all you have to do is set up "Google alerts" for any industry keywords and get cool stories sent to your inbox that you can share with your Twitter following.

- **20% Retweets of stuff the folks you've followed have posted**. Here's where you catch the attention of all those companies and recruiters. Retweet their stuff, perhaps with a quick thought of your own, and you WILL get noticed by those decision-makers in no time.

- **20% Fun Videos and/or pictures somewhat related to your industry**. You don't want to be boring. Videos and pics do well on Twitter. (Just keep them fam-friendly.) Good places for these include BuzzFeed, PopUrls and the Facebook account of any 15-year-old.

- **20% Your own blog posts**. Here's

where you share those little nuggets of awesomeness you create each week.

Now, I will not tell you HOW OFTEN you need to post on Twitter. That will depend on your available time, and affinity for Twitter.

Try to shoot for at least one to three times a day; ramping up as you get more followers and get some interesting discussions going with your followers.

Obviously the more you TWEET, the more RESULTS you get. And if you follow the formula above, soon you'll get tons of retweets, so when you contact somebody who has a job opening…

You won't be seen as some needy schmuck, but instead as an industry thought leader.

Twitter Pillar No.4: Put It On Autopilot

Here's where Twitter gets really exciting.

Unlike social platforms like Facebook, which

force you to consume all content in one fire hose of craziness, Twitter lets you organize, separate and schedule all of your Twitter activity into little silos of Twitter job-seeking magnificence.

And for this I turn to a tool called HootSuite.

It's FREE. It's easy. And it's an absolute MUST to handle all your new Twitter activity. You can even use the HootSuite dashboard to handle all your LinkedIn and Facebook stuff too.

So, how best can we use HootSuite for our job search duties? Here's how I've got it set up:

1. **Create a HootSuite account.**

2. **Link up your Twitter account and your HootSuite dashboard.** This will create a "tab" for your specific Twitter account.

3. **Schedule your tweets**. Except for the ReTweets. Those you must do as they happen.

4. **Create "streams" for job search #hashtags**. You do this by clicking "add stream" and then adding hashtags in the

"keyword" field. This would let you create bookmarked searches for tweets based on hashtags like #resume, #jobhunt, and #jobposting.

5. **Create "streams" based on industry-specific #hashtags and keywords.** The process is the same, only the keywords are different. This lets you chime in on any conversations happening in real-time.

6. **Create "streams" based on any industry-specific events or conferences.** Most events and conferences have some kind of #hashtag going. Just tap into the hashtag conversation and it'll be like you're there. Without all the bad hotel food and expensive parking.

I know. This sounds like a lot. It's NOT.

Once I've got my streams set up, I really only spend about 15-20 minutes a day checking my account, retweeting cool stuff, sharing my blog posts, and keeping up on the latest hashtag goodies.

Here's the cool thing: after a while people (including recruiters and hiring managers) will respond. And asking YOU questions. (Crazy, right?)

And if they have a job opening, they might even let you know about it before the world does.

Which can be better than all the business cards in the world.

Chapter 4 Key Takeaways:

- **Make sure your Twitter profile is completed…to completion**. That includes getting your name in the username, including your job pitch in your bio, plenty of keywords sprinkled throughout, and a link to your virtual resume.

- **Follow as many relevant Twitter profiles as you can**. Including - companies and businesses you'd like to work for, local recruiters, industry movers and shakers, and anybody who can help you in your job search.

- **Break up your Twitter content portfolio to keep things balances**. 20% Quotes, 20% Blog Posts & Articles, 20% Funny Videos & Pictures, 20% Retweets of users you're following on Twitter, and 20% Your Blog

Content.

- **Use a tool, like HootSuite, to automate things**. Schedule your tweets in advance, set up job search streams, and keep tabs on everything going on in your industry.

Chapter 5:

The Strange, Mysterious and Oddly Powerful LinkedIn Job Search

"A thousand fibers connect us, and among those fibers, our actions run as causes, and come back to us as effects."

-Herman Melville

If you're anything like me, you have a love/hate relationship with LinkedIn.

You know you SHOULD be on there. (Because everybody tells you you have to.)

I WAS on there. I had tried it for years and had little response or success…let alone any job leads.

Which is strange, considering I was touting:

- A half-assed, 50% complete LinkedIn profile
- Nearly 14 connections (15 on a good day)
- An intense regimen of logging in every three months

LinkedIn is an amazing and powerful networking tool — and full of hiring managers and recruiters and company decision-makers who fill positions all the time — but only if you put effort into it. (And use a couple of the awesome tools LinkedIn has to offer, and that barely anybody takes advantage of.)

So, next I will share my 6 Steps to Maximizing Your LinkedIn Presence to help you leverage this powerful networking tool to increase your leads and help you stand out in a crowded job market:

LinkedIn Step No.1: Get Thy Profile Looking Complete and Kick-Ass

Here's the nasty little secret about LinkedIn profiles: Most people don't finish theirs. Or if they do, they neglect vital elements which affect their discover-ability.

So here's my LinkedIn Profile checklist to get your LinkedIn "face" looking its absolute best:

- **Name:** Try your best to claim your REAL name. If taken, go with variations such as "The Real Michael Clarke" or "The Michael Clarke." (Insert YOUR name. That'd be weird if you used my name.)
- **Picture:** Use a real pic, please. No company logos, no screen grabs from your favorite video game. Just you.
- **Headline:** Tell 'em what you can offer. (And use keywords when possible.)

Don't put some dry headline, such as "Project Manager, XYZ Consulting." Instead, tell hiring managers who you are and what you've got in your toolbox: "Customer-Focused Marketing Manager - Responsible for 200% YOY Growth - Email Marketing Certified."

- **Summary:** Never leave this blank. If you do, I will come to your house and make you read through my pile of old resumes. Tell stories about your job experience and accomplishments (and use plenty of keywords). And for the love of all that is holy, please break up your summary into smaller paragraphs. (You ain't writing *War and Peace* here.)

- **Experience:** Focus on your accomplishments, not your tasks. Put in a current position even if you don't have one. (Remember you are NOW an industry blogger, so use that if you need.)

- **Recommendations:** Get at least three recommendations to get your profile to 100% completion. How do you do that? Well, first, you got to make connections…and that's what we will cover in the next step!

LinkedIn Step No.2: Connect With Every Living Human Being

Okay, maybe not EVERY human being, but as many as you can think of.

This is easy when you let LinkedIn access your email contacts to suggest connections. (Although you may get some random, and awkward, connection suggestions that way.)

Here's a quick list of folks to focus on when building out your LinkedIn network:

- Work colleagues, past and present (Dig deep here)
- Friends and family
- Previous clients
- The Company Pages of every business you've worked for (Unless it ended poorly)
- Folks on Twitter you've talked with

And once you've got about 40-50 connections there — builds up quickly — then go after:

- Recruiters in your area - just click on the LinkedIn advanced search and do a local search.
- Folks on Twitter (such as recruiters, hiring managers, or job search gurus) that you follow and would like to connect with.
- Company Pages of businesses you'd like to work for.

LinkedIn Step No.3: Join As Many Relevant Groups as Possible

This is where LinkedIn kicks ass.

No joke, the moment I stopped waiting for the world to visit my profile and offer me a job…

…the moment I got out there and joined groups and helped add to the conversation, my employment prospects changed.

That's because groups are tightly themed silos of awesomeness in the greater LinkedIn universe.

To find groups to join, just click on the "Interest" tab at the top of your LinkedIn dashboard, and choose the "Groups" drop-down. From there it's just a matter of searching by keyword, region or interest.

There is a limit to the number of groups you can join, but don't worry. Choose wisely, and that'll be all you need. (Forget paying for the LinkedIn Premium service that lets you join more groups. It ain't worth it.)

So, here are the KINDS of groups I think are a MUST for you to join:

- **Industry Groups:** This'll depend on what kind of job you're going for, but don't limit yourself here. Something as broad as marketing has so many sub-niche groups (social marketing, video marketing, etc.) you're bound to find something.

- **Alumni Groups:** If you graduated from any higher institution, no doubt they've got an alumni group. Don't forget community college or vocational schools. (If the group doesn't exist yet, you could always create it.)

- **Regional Groups:** Groups in your own backyard can range in quality and consistency, so you must do your homework. But there can be good leads there.

LinkedIn Step No.4: Give a Little Bit

Here's where the LinkedIn magic happens.

MOST job seekers on LinkedIn (like me, years ago) create their profile and WAIT.

Or if they don't wait, they send obnoxious messages to random strangers asking for recommendations and introductions. ("Hey, I know you don't know me. But can you introduce me to your friend…it would help ME out.")

If, instead, if you can show you care about more than just your OWN neurotic job search and help your fellow Group members in their own quest, then when a job opening comes up in your extended network you'll be the FIRST person they think of.

And how do you become a Most Favored LinkedIn Contact? By:

- **Asking and answering questions in your Groups**. I like to check in at least twice a week to all of my groups.

- **Give kudos to other people in the**

group who've accomplished something. People love them some recognition.

- **Answering questions in the "LinkedIn Answers" section**. This is a powerful little feature that anybody uses. Great way to boost your visibility.

- **Share those helpful blog posts you wrote in your Groups**. Don't overdo it. Once a week in each group is fine.

- **Share those same blogs posts in your status updates**. These will be seen by your existing network. Once that network builds up you'll see real movement with your content.

- **Help other people in their job search if you can**. This means: writing recommendations; giving intros to people you know, encouraging people, being an overall cool/supportive person, etc.

The first FIVE are all about building up your brand. Doing all of that will make your profile look so much more impressive than 99% of all the other LinkedIn schmucks out there.

The LAST ONE is about keeping the karma gods and goddesses happy. (Which is always a good thing to do.)

LinkedIn Step No.5: Go on the Hunt

Once you've done the first FOUR for a while, then you're ready for the FINAL SHOWDOWN.

You're ready to reach out to companies, recruiters, connections, total (somewhat) strangers to see if they could help you in your goal of finding a full-time gig.

Do this step before you nail down the first four and your chances at success will diminish.

Having the foundation of a killer profile, lots of connections, tons of group activity, and a robust level of network interaction and you will

be poised to be seen not just as a candidate…but as the ONLY candidate.

So, here's how I recommend you approach the whole LinkedIn Job Hunt process:

- **Start with the LinkedIn job board.** Lot of people don't even know LinkedIn has their own proprietary job board, with tons of listings.

- **Target the 2nd and 3rd degree connection of companies you'd like to approach.** These are friends of friends who might work at a specific company you want an interview with, or they may be in a position to look at your resume.

- **Reach out to recruiters to see if they have any openings.** You should already have a list of these from your Twitter and LinkedIn searches. (And if you've been a frequent content sharer, this will set you apart from the masses.)

- **Connect with friends/connections who've moved to a new job**. See if they know of anything cooking on their side of the fence. Nobody recruits like a new employee.
- **Pose a question in your Groups to see if anybody knows about any openings**. It's vital you do this AFTER you've already contributed to the group.

The key is to make sure you don't sound desperate or overbearing. Just sound like the relaxed, awesome person you are.

Everybody knows what it's like to look for a job. But the more you can make it a "fun" experience for the person helping you out, the better off will be.

I do something like:

"Hey Jim,

Saw your post about what Britney Spears can teach us about Social Media Marketing. Loved it! (Had me humming "Hit Me Baby One More Time" for the rest of the day.

That's a good thing, right?)

    So, I had a question. In my quest to take over the world — i.e.: nail a marketing associate position — I noticed you're connected with Tom Knoble over at Illumina Ltd.

    Would you mind forwarding an intro to him from me? I promise not to embarrass myself. (And that includes singing any Britney Spears. Unless you think it would help.)

    Thanks so much. And talk soon,

    Michael"

Notice how:

- **I gave him kudos for something he did**. It's not all about me.)
- **I kept it light.** (Or as light as a Britney Spears reference can get.)
- **I asked him to "forward an intro."** I didn't ask him to write me a recommendation or pen an essay. Just forward something. Super easy.
- **I assured him I wouldn't make him look bad**. This is big. Don't forget this

part.

Be funny, somewhat self-deprecating…and you'll find your connections will be happy to help you in whatever way possible. (And give you the chance to leverage those relationships into the full-time gig of your dreams.)

Chapter 5 Key Takeaways:

- **It's SUPER important to get your LinkedIn profile to 100% completion and looking snazzy.** This means - a) Every field filled out b) At least three recommendations c) Kick-ass accomplishments in the summary d) A catchy job pitch in the headline and e) Tons of industry keywords sprinkled throughout.

- **Connect with all friends, family, colleagues** (past and present) and social media contacts you can think of.

- **Groups are SUPER key to connecting on a grand scale**. Join as many industry, regional and alumni groups you can find.

- **You gotta GIVE in the form of comments, likes, link shares,** and your own content before you can expect to get anything out of a group.

- **Once you've established a foundation of awesomeness**, then you can - ask your groups and existing network if they know about any openings, ask contacts to forward an intro to key decision-makers, and contact recruiters to see if they got anything on their end.

Chapter 6:

How Facebook Can Help You "Like" Your Way to a New Career

"A friend is somebody who knows all about you, and still loves you."

-Elbert Hubbard

Most job seekers KNOW LinkedIn is a powerful career networking tool. (Even if they screw up their presence on it.)

But Facebook is an often-overlooked part of the

career search quest.

Which is too bad because Facebook:

- **Has a ton of eyeballs.** (One billion and counting)
- **Has tons of cool job search apps** built onto their platform.
- **Has dedicated company pages for any industry** or business you want to work for.
- **Has so much demographic data it's scary**. (Which makes it a helluva lot easier to connect with people who can get you an interview.)
- **Is the ONE social network that everybody uses**. (Including your grandma in Paducah, Kentucky who might just KNOW one HR professional at that company you want to work for.)

Now, with great power comes great responsibility. It's possible, if not done properly, to "status update" your way to Facebook job oblivion. (Not to mention piss off a bunch of your friends and family.)

But don't worry that's what Uncle Benjamin's here for.

So, here are my 5 Steps to Facebook Job-Search Domination:

Facebook Job-Search Step No.1: Give Your Profile a Makeover

This doesn't mean spending hundreds of dollars on pretty graphics for your profile. (Though if you want to…)

No, instead I'd like you to:

- **Remove all pictures, status updates, and shared links that are dubious**. We mentioned this in Chapter 2. But it bears repeating: Your profile is the FIRST thing most prospective employers look at. Give your profile the Soft Scrub treatment and remove any questionable stuff.

- **Include everything you can think of in the "Professional Skills" field of your profile**. This will make you much easier to find on the Facebook search listings. As always, keywords are…key!

- **Update your work experience if needed**. You won't be able to "edit" the company pages for your previous jobs. (Usually) But you can add projects you were a part of. Again, try to get in keywords, if possible.

- **Get a cool (and cheap) Timeline cover for your profile**. Head over to Fiverr.com to get somebody to make you one for just a couple of bucks. (You could include things like quotes, sayings, mantras, your particular skills, etc.) Here's a cool collection of Facebook

Timeline cover photos
(JobSamurai.org/FbookCovers) to use
as inspiration.

Facebook Job-Search Step No.2: Connect With…Everyone!

No matter how many "friends" you already have on Facebook, you can always have more. Those include:

- **All your email contacts**. (Both personal and professional.)
- **Former work colleagues**. Especially managers and bosses. (That you're still speaking to.)
- **Folks you went to school with.** Fellow alumnus can be a fantastic source of job leads.
- **Any recruiters you've worked with in**

the past. (Even if it didn't lead to a gig.)

- **Any acquaintances in your other social media networks**. This includes Twitter, LinkedIn, GoodReads…whatever! I once got an interview by adding a recruiter from my Shelfari world to my Facebook world. (Weird, but true.)

Facebook Job-Search Step No.3: Follow Pages, Join Groups

In case you're not up on your Facebook terminology: Facebook pages (officially called "Fan Pages") are public company pages that anybody can "like" and "follow."

As a "fan" you are more likely to see that Page's status updates in your newsfeed. Also as a fan, you may or may not be able to post a status update on that given page. (This will depend on the setting that the Page Admin decides upon.)

Facebook groups are private groups that require an admin to grant access. Like Fan Pages, members see group messages in their newsfeed. But they are not as common as Fan Pages.

They both have their pros and cons. Here's how I suggest approaching these with your job search:

PAGES

Try to follow Fan Pages associated with:

- Companies you want to work for
- Companies you worked for (Helps you reconnect with old colleagues)
- University and high school pages you're an alumnus of
- Industries you're a part of or hope to be a part of (There's a lot of these. Keep digging until you find them all)
- Staffing Agencies that cover your area
- Recruiters that cover your area
- Resources or vendors that your ideal company might follow (For instance,

say I wanted to work as a golf instructor. Then I might follow pages that cater to golf course designers and owners.)

GROUPS

Try to follow groups associated with:

- Your industry (Regional is always best.)
- Your interests and hobbies (These can be good sources of job leads.)
- University and high school pages you're an alumnus of

This will take time. But finding these groups and Pages can lead to some of the best job leads you'll find on Facebook.

Facebook Job-Search Step No.4: Embrace Your Inner App

These ain't the apps you install on your

smartphone and crash every few minutes. (I curse you, Apple Maps!)

Facebook apps are applications that let you interface with certain web tools from your Facebook profile.

Yeah, they ask for permission to get access to your list of contacts. (It's not that big a deal, unless your contacts are living off the grid in some compound in Montana.)

Now some of these will come and go. (I used to recommend JobVite until they were bought by a recruiting start-up. Pesky recruiters.)

But the one that is still going strong that I recommend you install as soon as possible.

- Social Jobs Partnership: Probably the best job search app in the whole Facebook universe. (Probably because Facebook helped create it.) Comprehensive and easy-to-use, this app is a definite add to your toolbox.

Facebook Job Search Step No.5: Comment, Share, Pester

Okay, maybe not pester.

How about gently "remind?"

Truth is, your ability to connect with folks who have the job you want will be tied to how much Facebook interaction you have.

And that all comes down to:

- Shares
- Likes
- Comments

Now this might come easy for you. You may already spend 20 hours a day commenting, liking, and sharing on Facebook. If so, then you're already plugged in and good to go.

But if you're like me, who sees the popularity of Facebook as a sign of the zombie apocalypse, then you must re-engage with the human race and start "caring" and "sharing" about your extended network.

And the easiest way to do that is to:

- "Like" stuff your friends post (Creates "affinity" with your connections, which Facebook uses to calculate popularity.)
- Make comments
- "Share" cool photos AND videos (And your own blog posts.)

Here's how I break it down:

Every day (Between 10am-12pm)

- I look for TWO things: a funny video or photo (check PopUrls or BuzzFeed for these) AND an interesting story or blog related to my industry. (Google Alerts and AllTop are great places for these.)

Every day (Between 4pm-6pm)

- Post my "funny" photo or video as a status update on my personal profile.

- Scan, like, and comment on any new activity in my newsfeed from my personal connections.
- Post my "industry" story on any relevant Facebook Fan Pages and Groups.
- Scan, like and comment on any new activity in my groups and Pages.

Wednesdays (Between 4pm-6pm)

- Post your BLOG POST to your Main newsfeed. Ask for "likes" and "shares."
- Post your BLOG POST to all relevant Fan Pages & Groups. Thank people for reading and ask them to leave a comment in the box below.

The reason we target Wednesday is that it's the BIGGEST traffic day of the week on Facebook.

But notice how, when thrown into the general mix of your weekly Facebook duties, it seems less like overt self-promotion, and more like adding to the conversation.

Which it is. It so happens to be one of the best business cards.

This one tactic alone will bring your name — and your resume — to the top of your industry's slush pile in no time.

Facebook Job-Search Tip No.6: Close the Deal

So what do you do after upping your Facebook engagement and broadening your network of "friends?" How do you turn all those Facebook allies into actual job leads?

Well, Facebook requires more subtlety than the other social networks when promoting your skills; most people resent overt promo stuff on there.

Once you've built up your Facebook cred, and have a ton of people who can help spread and share your stuff, here are a couple ways to leverage your network and get some real job possibilities out of it.

- **Share your job search experience. (But in a funny way.)** Leave the gory, depressing stuff for your therapist. But if something humorous happens during an interview, phone screener or job fair, share it. It's a nice subtle way of reminding people you're on the market.

- **Ask for people to SHARE your blog content. (Especially if they know somebody in your industry.)** You'd be surprised how many people know each other, and one simple share of your content could be the one thing you need to make a crucial connection.

- **Ask for people's advice about specific areas of your job search**. Whenever I'm confused about something in the job search quest — such as "How to dress for an interview with a super casual company" — I'll ask my Facebook inner circle. Not only does it get a bunch of comments, but it's another sneaky way of reminding people that: "Hey! This guy needs a job, you know."

- **Ask if anybody KNOWS somebody at a certain company**. You never want to ask your Facebook peeps: "Hey...anybody got a job for me?" But asking if anybody knows anybody at a specific company is acceptable and can be a super-efficient way to cut through the usual company gatekeepers.

Chapter 6 Key Takeaways:

- **Clean up your Facebook profile before using it to boost your job search**. Remove controversial status updates, racy photos, and update your professional skills.

- **Add as many people as you can to your existing Facebook network.** This includes friends & family, former colleagues, and social-media buddies.

- **"Like" relevant pages and join relevant groups** to expand your Facebook reach.

- **JobVite and Social Jobs Partnership are two Facebook apps every job seeker should have in their Facebook dashboard**. These apps let you search from open job listings, right from your Facebook profile.

- **The best way to "up" your Facebook

engagement level is to like, share and comment. Try to share your own content on Wednesdays, the biggest Facebook engagement day of the week.

- **Sharing funny anecdotes about your job search, or asking for advice and feedback, can be great ways** to engage with your Facebook peeps, and remind them you could use help in the job department.

Chapter 7:

Super-Advanced Cool Ninja Job Search Tricks

"The best way out, is always through."

-Robert Frost

It's my hope you won't need any of the strategies in this chapter.

It's my hope that by following the strategies in the first six chapters, you'll have so many contacts, leads and good job offers you'll never have to read these words.

But, alas, as long as Wall Street continues to

screw up the Western economy — and Kim Kardashian continues to be one of the most highly paid celebrities (or whatever she is) in the world — I can't be sure about anything.

And that includes what will help you break through and land that killer job you've been aiming for.

So, consider this your Post-graduate program, your Ph.D. in Job-Search Studies. Here are SEVEN super-advanced Ninja job search tricks that are effective, ruthless, and I can guarantee NOBODY else is doing. (And that includes your competition.)

Ninja Trick No.1: Press Releases

Press releases? But aren't those for…oh, I don't know…newsworthy things?

First off, if you could see the utter junk that people write press releases about, you wouldn't for a second think twice about publishing a press release.

Second…you ARE doing some newsworthy!

You are writing BLOG POSTS about your industry. And each of those posts/entries make up ANOTHER chance for you to get your name out there:

- *"Sacramento Financial Planner Offers Plan to Solve Washington Debt"*
- *"Denver IT Professional Explains How to Keep the NSA From Bugging Your Phone"*
- *"Omaha Fitness Trainer Shares 3 Tips for Getting a Hollywood Body"*

See, how I got in a tabloid/current-event angle and got in the whole [city/occupation] thing in there.

It's possible with a well-placed press release you could show up on the first page of Google for something like "Denver accountant."

Writing the press release is easy. Just regurgitate the main aspects of your blog post. Here's a FREE template from HubSpot on how to write a "presser" — as they call them in the biz. (JobSamurai.org/HubPress)

But PAY for the actual distribution of the press release.

There are a ton of companies that do this. From the ultra-expensive (PR WEB~$300) to the ultra-budget (Web Wire ~ $30).

But because I know money is tight when you're on the job search, I'm offering a special for readers of my book. I'll send your press release out through my press release service I've got set up with a company called SB Wire, for $7 a pop. Nearly 75% of what it would cost you, with a ton more distribution.

Ninja Trick No.2: Facebook Ads

Remember when I told you that Facebook had all this amazing demographic data just sitting there on its servers. Well, you can use all that invasive, privacy-killing data for your own job-search benefit.

Just create a Facebook ad campaign with a small daily budget — couple bucks a day should do it —

by clicking on the "wheel" at the top right of your Facebook profile and clicking "Create an ad."

Cool thing is, with a Facebook ad you can target people by:

- City
- Occupation (Such as "hiring manager" or "recruiter")
- Company (Great, if you know which companies you'd like to work for)
- Which Facebook pages a person Has "Liked" (If there's a page your industry decision-makers follow, this can be a super sneaky way in.)
- Education (Great for alumni connections)
- Precise Interests

…or any combination of these!

Now, the more targeted you are with your campaign, the more you must pay. But we're talking about a few pennies per click, and the leads you get will be so targeted that it'll be worth it

So what do you put in your ad? Well, here's my down-and-dirty tips for creating a Facebook ad:

- **Have the headline be a question**. Questions force the brain to engage, and you want them to engage. Some examples: "Looking for an ambitious Maine graphic designer?"; "Searching for a SEO expert in Houston?" "Need a Smart, Hard-working Admin Assistant?"

- **Use your picture as the creative image for the headline**. Go with a headshot, one that makes you look somewhat professional and not like a psychopath.

- **Keep the body text simple**. Something like - "I'm Dave. I'm a Minneapolis web designer who's agile, dedicated, a huge Vikings fan…and not afraid to do whatever it takes to help your company succeed."

- **Link over to your virtual resume, or your blog**. Don't just link over to your Facebook Timeline. Although you could link over to a Facebook custom app with your resume. It's more technical, but well worth doing.

- **Set up your Facebook ad campaign on a CPM (Cost per 1000 impressions) basis, as opposed to a CPC (Cost per click) basis**. This means you're paying for eyeballs, as opposed to paying per click. This will keep you from spending a ton of money on your ad.

- **Pause your ad at night**. You need not run your ad when nobody is on Facebook. Just click "pause" in the Facebook ad dashboard and then click "resume" again in the morning.

- **Put in a bid price about .6 or .7 cents**

over the minimum bid. Don't do the recommend bid. That's for suckers. Keep it low, but not too low.

Ninja Trick No.3: Ezine and Newsletter Ads

Facebook ain't the only place you can buy ads to boost your job-searching potential.

From $10-$100 you can create a dedicated Ezine or newsletter ad touting your skills — and your ability to contribute to a business — that reaches thousands of would-be decision makers.

Now, you must do legwork to find that perfect Ezine or newsletter for your industry. The Ezine Directory is a great resource to find locations for your ad. You could also do a Google search of: "[your industry]" AND "newsletter" to see what comes up.

I've found smaller newsletter/Ezine publishers

are VERY open to negotiating ad rates. Translation: it's a real pain to sell ads and most of them have plenty of ad inventory to sell.

Some newsletters may even segment their list by geographic region, meaning you're reaching ONLY the people who can make a dent in your job search.

What do you say in the ad?

Well, it DEPENDS on the industry. But as with any advertising, the KEY is to approach it from the mind of the person reading it.

What would make somebody checks their Ezine newsletter to click over and check out my resume, blog post, website, etc.?

Here's one I used a couple years back:

Headline: *"Direct Response Marketing Copywriter Discovers the Secret to Selling More Merch"*

(Notice how I didn't say: "Copywriter Needs a Job!" or "I'm Awesome…Here's How!" Nobody cares about you. Yet.)

"Most sales gurus say people buy ANYTHING for one

of two reasons: a) To take away pain or b) To gain pleasure.

"Most sales gurus are wrong. To find out the REAL secret reason most people buy ANYTHING, and boost your conversions, check out my NEW report on the Direct Response industry…"

Then I linked over to a blog post where I talked about the REAL reason people buy. (Which also included info about how I was available for freelance or full-time gigs in the sidebar widget.)

Notice how I enticed them with something that benefits them and used a bunch of industry-specific lingo ("merch," "direct response," "conversions") that shows them I speak their language. (I'm one of them; they can trust me.)

It worked like gangbusters. I got twenty-two emails. Which led to nine phone interviews. Which led to six in-person interviews…

…which led to two offers…

..which led to a frickin' job!

Ninja Trick No.4: Conquering the Job Market With YouTube

I hesitated to even add this one as most people would rather be set on fire than actually talk to other humans on camera.

But…YouTube is a staggeringly effective way to build your credibility and get you in front of thousands of possible job leads in a matter of a few weeks.

This is because:

- **YouTube videos rank much higher in the search-engine results** than individual blog posts.
- **YouTube is the second-largest search engine in the world.** Meaning there are a lot of eyeballs on there.
- **Video is a great way to SHOW off your personality.** Or at least show you have one.

- **Your competition is NOT doing this**. Trust me.

So, what do you shoot videos about? Simple, just take your blog posts and turn them into videos.

Now, you don't have to create Hollywood-level presentations, but I recommend you invest in some kind of external microphone. (Radio Shack should have all the adapters you need for less than $25.)

Trust me: *bad audio is much worse than bad video*.

Here's what I do when creating my videos:

- **Set up my iPhone on a book case**. On its side, this ensures you get a good aspect ratio.

- **Plug in my external microphone.**

- **Start the video off by telling folks what I'm gonna talk about**. For example - "In this video I will talk about How to Get More Fans for Your Facebook Page."

- **Repeat the main points covered in**

my blog post. Need not memorize it, just go off-the-cuff.

- **Finish up by encouraging people to "click on the link below to check out my blog."**
- **Upload the video to YouTube**. Don't forget to use the editing feature in YouTube to cut out all the "umms" and "aaahs."
- **Use the title of your blog post as the title for the video**.
- **Include a link to your blog in the video description**. (Be sure to include the "http://" part.)

And that's it! You're good to go.

And before you know it you'll get a ton of new job leads you never thought possible. You might even get a few speaking gigs out of it. I know I did.

Chapter 7 Key Takeaways:

- **Press releases are effective for promoting you and the content you publish**. Good old Benjamin has a deal for ya if wanna send one. Ping me over at ben@jobsamurai.com.

- **Facebook ads are scary targeted ways to reach hiring folks.** You can target by demographic, company, interests, page likes…anything!

- **Keep your Facebook ads simple**. Short text, question headlines, close-up images, and a link over to your blog and resume.

- **Ezines and newsletters are great ways to reach people looking to add talent to their team.** "Sell" the benefit of your expertise in your blog post, not your hire-ability, and then "close" them over on your blog.

- **YouTube videos are frightening; they are also fantastic ways to reach a ton of industry insiders.** Just reiterate the main points of a blog post and provide a link to your blog in the video description.

Epilogue:

Next Stop, World Domination

"If you want something new, you have to stop doing something old."

-Peter Drucker

We've talked a lot about finding a job in this book. (I would hope so, given the title: Finding a Job in the 21st Century.)

If finding a stable, structured 9-5 (or even longer) gig is all you're looking for, then let me say I TRULY hope that some tips in this book have been helpful.

Much of what I shared in this book has been

from personal experience, and hard-earned wisdom.

Not to mention a sneaky suspicion that building your brand, in the ways we've gone over, is the ultimate long-term employment strategy…not fancier resumes.

And yet…

I'd like to plant a seed in your crazy, wonderful brain.

All the strategies we've gone over are the same ones that entrepreneurs and tech start-ups and authors and public speakers and consultants use to build their expert reputation. (Which lead to HUGE paydays.)

Because people (and the companies they run) will ALWAYS pay for somebody who *knows more than they do in an area of expertise* that helps them save time, make more money, feel better, or gets rid of pain.

And they will pay. (I know. I quit my job because I was making more money as a freelance consultant than I was as a full-time wage slave.)

So, as you go forward in your job search, keep

an eye on that horizon just out of reach.

While you may have no interest in starting your own business or creating your own company — and I didn't either — just remember, the only things you can depend on in a job market is uncertainty and your own talents.

It's my hope that this book has helped you claim some of the kick-ass talent potential I know you have just waiting to get started.

And if you'd like to drop me a line and let me know what you thought of my book, send me an email over at ben@jobsamurai.org.

Good luck and don't let the Monster applications get you down!

DISCLAIMER AND/OR LEGAL NOTICES:
Every effort has been made to accurately represent this book and it's potential. Results vary with every individual, and your results may or may not be different from those depicted. No promises, guarantees or warranties, whether stated or implied, have been made that you will produce any specific result from this book. Your efforts are individual and unique, and may vary from those shown. Your success depends on your efforts, background and motivation.

The material in this publication is provided for educational and informational purposes only and is not intended as business advice. Use of the programs, advice, and information contained in this book is at the sole choice and risk of the reader.

CPSIA information can be obtained
at www.ICGtesting.com
Printed in the USA
LVHW081803221119
638114LV00016BA/1609/P